THE HYPERTECT

EARL S. BELL, ASSOC. AIA
Copyright 2024 by BG Latitude LLC, New York
ALL RIGHTS RESERVED

HYPERTECT BY EARL S BELL

Introduction

Prologue

In the realm of design and construction, a silent revolution has been brewing. As the dawn of the 21st century broke, it became increasingly clear that the traditional silos of architecture, engineering, and technology were no longer sufficient in addressing the complex challenges of our rapidly evolving world. The need for a radical rethinking of how we create our built environment led to the birth of a new vision: the fusion of diverse disciplines into a singular, harmonious symphony of design and functionality. This vision gave birth to a new era in construction and design, heralding the rise of the Building Design Scientist or "Hypertect."

The journey to this transformation was neither sudden nor arbitrary. It was the culmination of years of technological advancements, the merging of cross-disciplinary knowledge, and a growing awareness of our impact on the environment. The seeds of this change were planted by the pioneers of the past – the polymaths like Filippo Brunelleschi and Imhotep, who saw no boundaries between art, science, and engineering. Their legacy whispered through the centuries, inspiring a new generation of thinkers and builders who dared to dream of a world where the creation of space was not just an act of construction but a dance of interwoven expertise.

At the heart of this evolution lies the revolutionary integration of Building Information Modeling (BIM) and Artificial Intelligence (AI). BIM's ability to create a detailed and adaptable 3D model of a building project revolutionized how architects and engineers collaborate and visualize their work. AI further propelled this transformation, offering unprecedented insights through data analysis, predictive modeling, and automated design processes. Together, they form the backbone of Building Design Science, enabling the creation of structures that are not only aesthetically pleasing but also intelligent, sustainable, and in harmony with their environment.

Yet, as with any revolution, the path was fraught with challenges. Traditional industry practices resisted change, professional boundaries were called into question, and regulatory frameworks struggled to keep pace with innovation. The emergence of the Building Design Scientist as a profession demanded new education paradigms, a rethinking of licensing norms, and a collaborative approach that transcended established disciplines.

This book is a journey through that transformative process. It is a narrative of how the built environment is evolving, of how a new breed of professionals is reshaping the landscape of architecture and engineering, and of how technology is becoming an inseparable part of design and construction. As you turn these pages, you will discover the convergence of architecture, structural engineering, MEP engineering, and AI technology. You will explore the global race among jurisdictions to lead in this new field, the economic implications, the challenges of integrating new laws, and the future that Building Design Science promises.

Welcome to the future of building design – a future where the legacy of the Hypertect is just beginning to unfold, where the boundaries of imagination are constantly expanding, and where the creation of space is a testament to human ingenuity and the relentless pursuit of progress.

The future is not just being built; it is being designed with a vision that transcends time and disciplines. Welcome to the era of the Building Design Scientist. Welcome to the world of Hypertecture.

Table of Contents

F

CHAPTER 1

Chapter 1: The Birth of a Vision

1.1 Introduction

In an era where boundaries between disciplines blur and the quest for innovation reaches new heights, the field of architecture and engineering is undergoing a profound transformation. This chapter introduces a groundbreaking concept: the amalgamation of Architecture with the AEC professions along with AI technology, also known as BDS or Hypertecture; Hypertect / Hypertecture is a term coined by Earl S Bell. It marks a paradigm shift, where the fusion of diverse disciplines promises to reshape the very fabric of the built environment. This journey of exploration delves into the emergence of this visionary approach, bridging traditional practices with futuristic innovations.

1.2 From Architecture to Building Design Science (BDS) / Hypertecture

The evolution from conventional architectural practices to Building Design Science (BDS) or Hypertecture represents more than a mere change; it signifies a radical reimagining of the field. This section traces the journey from the foundations of architectural design to its expansion into a more holistic, integrated discipline. It examines how the incorporation of structural engineering, MEP (Mechanical, Electrical, and Plumbing) engineering, along with the cutting-edge insights provided by AI technologists, is reshaping the role of architects and engineers. BDS or Hypertecture emerges as a multidisciplinary realm, breaking down long-standing silos and fostering a new, comprehensive approach to building design.

1.3 The Convergence: Architecture, Structural Engineering, MEP Engineering, and AI Technologists

At the heart of BDS/Hypertecture lies the convergence of several distinct fields: architecture, structural engineering, MEP engineering, and AI technology. This subsection delves into how this collaborative melding is revolutionizing the design and construction process. It highlights the unique contributions of each discipline and how their integration leads to innovative, efficient, and more adaptive building solutions. The convergence is not just about technical collaboration; it represents the emergence of a new breed of professionals—Building Design Scientists—who possess a holistic understanding and capability to address the multifaceted challenges of modern architecture.

1.4 Historical Roots: Resurrecting the Polymath Professional

Understanding the future of BDS/Hypertecture requires a look back at history's polymath professionals. This section pays homage to the likes of Filippo Brunelleschi and Imhotep, whose work transcended the confines of singular disciplines. By examining their holistic approach to building design, we draw parallels and gather inspiration for the modern era of Hypertecture. These historical figures demonstrate the power and potential of integrating diverse fields of knowledge, setting a precedent for today's Building Design Scientists. The legacy of these polymaths is not only preserved but also revitalized in the contemporary pursuit of integrated, innovative design solutions.

This first chapter lays a comprehensive foundation for understanding Building Design Science, its significance, and its roots, setting the tone for an in-depth exploration of this innovative field in the subsequent chapters.

CHAPTER 2

Chapter 2: The Building Design Scientist / Hypertect

2.1 Defining the Hypertect: A New Breed of Professional

The emergence of the 'Hypertect' marks a significant milestone in the evolution of building design. This new breed of professional embodies a synthesis of diverse skills and knowledge, reflecting the growing complexity and interdisciplinarity of modern architecture and engineering. The Hypertect is not just an architect, engineer, or technologist but a hybrid professional who seamlessly blends these roles.

Characteristics of a Hypertect: Central to the Hypertect's role is their adeptness in navigating and integrating architectural design, structural engineering, MEP engineering, and the application of AI technologies. This section delves into the specific skills and competencies that set the Hypertect apart, such as advanced problem-solving, creative innovation, and the ability to utilize AI and BIM tools effectively.

Role in Modern Design and Construction: The Hypertect's role in modern building design goes beyond mere construction. They are visionaries who foresee and address environmental, societal, and technical challenges through innovative design solutions. This part of the chapter will explore how Hypertects are reshaping the built environment, contributing to sustainable, efficient, and aesthetically appealing structures.

2.2 Education Revolution: Blurring the Lines Between Disciplines

The rise of the Hypertect has necessitated a revolution in educational approaches. Traditional silos in architectural and engineering education are giving way to a more integrated, interdisciplinary model.

Interdisciplinary Curriculum: This section examines how universities and educational institutions are restructuring their curricula to cater to the emerging needs of Building Design Science. It explores new teaching methodologies, course structures, and collaborative learning environments that blend architectural design, engineering principles, and technological training.

Training for Future Hypertects: Training programs and modules specifically designed for aspiring Hypertects are discussed. These programs aim not only to impart technical knowledge but also to foster creativity, innovation, and a holistic understanding of the built environment.

2.3 Examining the Ancient Polymaths: Filippo Brunelleschi and Imhotep

To fully appreciate the concept of the Hypertect, one must look back at the polymathic figures of history, like Filippo Brunelleschi and Imhotep, who exemplified multidisciplinary mastery in their work.

Legacy of Brunelleschi and Imhotep: This part of the chapter explores the contributions of these historical figures. Brunelleschi, known for his work on the Florence Cathedral, and Imhotep, the architect of the Step Pyramid, are studied for their innovative approaches that combined engineering, architecture, and other fields of knowledge.

Inspirations for Modern Hypertects: The chapter discusses how the principles and practices of these ancient polymaths can inspire and inform the modern Hypertect. It draws parallels between their work and the contemporary challenges faced by Hypertects, emphasizing the timeless value of interdisciplinary expertise.

2.4 Professional License Evolution: A Comprehensive Exam for the Building Design Scientist

As the profession of the Hypertect takes shape, there is a growing need for a revised licensing process that recognizes their unique skill set and knowledge base.

Development of a New Licensing Exam: The chapter details the development of a comprehensive licensing exam for Building Design Scientists. This exam aims to test a candidate's proficiency across multiple disciplines, including architectural design, engineering, and the application of AI in building design.

Implications for the Profession: The introduction of this new licensing system is a pivotal moment for the profession. It not only legitimizes the role of the Hypertect but also sets a standard for the knowledge and skills required to practice in this field. The section will discuss the potential impact of this change on professional practice, industry standards, and the future trajectory of building design.

Conclusion of Chapter 2:

In conclusion, Chapter 2 paints a comprehensive picture of the Building Design Scientist/Hypertect. It encapsulates the essence of this emerging professional, the transformative educational approaches that support their development, the historical roots that inspire their multidisciplinary approach, and the evolving professional landscape that recognizes and legitimizes their role. As a new chapter in the story of building design, the Hypertect stands as a symbol of innovation, integration, and the boundless potential of collaborative expertise in shaping the future of our built environment.

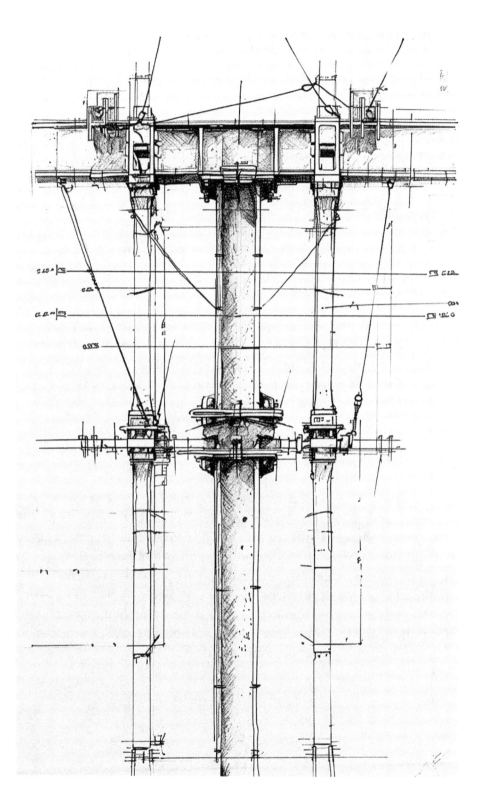

CHAPTER 3

Chapter 3: Technological Infusion: AI and BIM

3.1 Artificial Intelligence in Building Design Science

In the contemporary landscape of Building Design Science, Artificial Intelligence (AI) stands as a transformative force. This section explores the depth and breadth of AI's integration into building design, revolutionizing traditional methodologies.

AI's role extends from the initial conceptualization stages to the final execution of design. It introduces capabilities like predictive analytics, which forecast the potential successes and challenges of a design based on historical data and current trends. AI also plays a pivotal role in generative design, where algorithms generate a diverse range of design options based on specified criteria, pushing the boundaries of human creativity.

Moreover, AI contributes significantly to sustainability efforts in building design. Through intelligent analysis of environmental data, AI aids in creating structures that are energy-efficient, resource-conscious, and environmentally friendly. This section will provide detailed insights into how AI algorithms analyze and interpret vast datasets, offering solutions that are not only innovative but also sustainable.

The integration of AI in Building Design Science marks a new era of collaboration between human expertise and machine intelligence. By augmenting the capabilities of architects and engineers, AI paves the way for more advanced, accurate, and sustainable building designs.

3.2 Building Information Modeling (BIM) as the Central Hub

Building Information Modeling (BIM) has become the linchpin in the wheel of Building Design Science, evolving beyond a mere design tool into a comprehensive platform for project management. This subsection examines the transformative role of BIM as it becomes the central hub connecting various aspects of building design.

BIM facilitates a seamless integration of architectural design, structural engineering, and MEP engineering, enabling multidisciplinary teams to collaborate efficiently. It allows for real-time updates, shared access to models and data, and a unified platform for all stakeholders. The section will delve into the nuances of how BIM enhances the design process, from conceptualization to construction, and even post-construction management.

The narrative will also explore BIM's role in revolutionizing client-architect interactions. Through BIM's visualization capabilities, clients can now have a more immersive understanding of projects, leading to more informed decision-making. This subsection will provide case studies demonstrating BIM's efficacy in improving design quality, reducing construction errors, and streamlining project timelines.

3.3 Centralized Small Teams: Modeling Architecture, Structural Engineering, and MEP Engineering

The shift toward centralized small teams in building design represents a significant departure from traditional, compartmentalized approaches. This subsection explores the advantages of this paradigm shift, highlighting how it fosters efficiency, innovation, and cohesion in the design process.

Centralized teams, consisting of architects, engineers, and technologists, work collaboratively in a shared digital space, often facilitated by tools like BIM. This arrangement allows for rapid communication, seamless exchange of ideas, and an integrated approach to problem-solving. The section will delve into the dynamics of these teams, discussing how they leverage diverse expertise to tackle complex design challenges effectively.

Furthermore, this approach reduces the risk of miscommunication and errors, leading to a more streamlined and cost-effective design process. The narrative will include examples of successful projects achieved through this collaborative model, showcasing the tangible benefits of centralized small teams in modern building design.

3.4 Quantum Leap: Real-world Simulations and Digital Twins

The integration of quantum computing in Building Design Science marks a quantum leap in the field's capabilities. This subsection focuses on the groundbreaking potential of real-world simulations and the creation of digital twins, enabled by quantum computing's unparalleled computational power.

Digital twins, which are virtual replicas of physical buildings, allow for continuous monitoring and optimization of building performance. They represent a significant advancement in building lifecycle management, providing insights that can lead to enhanced sustainability, efficiency, and occupant comfort. This section will explore the use of digital twins in various stages of the building process, from design to maintenance.

Quantum computing enables the simulation of complex designs under a myriad of real-world conditions. These simulations allow architects and engineers to test and refine their designs in ways previously unimaginable. The section will discuss how this technology is pushing the boundaries of architectural design, enabling more resilient, adaptable, and visionary built environments.

Conclusion of Chapter 3:

In conclusion, Chapter 3 encapsulates the pivotal role of technological advancements in reshaping Building Design Science. From the deep integration of AI in enhancing design capabilities to BIM's role as a central hub for collaboration, and the revolutionary impact of quantum computing in simulations and digital twins, this chapter illustrates a future where technology is inextricably linked with every aspect of building design and construction. These advancements herald a new age of efficiency, precision, and sustainability in the built environment, emphasizing the transformative power of technological infusion in the field of architecture and engineering.

CHAPTER 4

Chapter 4: Transforming the Profession

4.1 Financial Impact: Higher Average Salaries and Cost Efficiency

The emergence of Building Design Science, particularly the role of the Hypertect, is significantly impacting the financial landscape of the architecture and engineering industries. This section delves deep into how this paradigm shift is leading to higher average salaries for professionals and overall cost efficiencies in design and construction projects.

Elevating Earning Potentials: The comprehensive skill set and expertise of the Hypertect in AI, BIM, and integrated design processes significantly enhance their market value. This section examines the factors contributing to the increased earning potential, supported by industry salary surveys and economic analyses.

Cost Efficiency in Projects: The integration of multidisciplinary knowledge and advanced technologies leads to more efficient design processes, reducing costs in both the short and long term. This part of the chapter will provide examples of projects where these efficiencies have been realized, showcasing cost savings in design, construction, and building maintenance.

Economic Analysis: A detailed economic analysis highlighting the ROI (Return on Investment) of implementing Building Design Science principles in construction projects. This analysis will include case studies demonstrating the financial benefits for both clients and design firms.

Changing Salary Dynamics: A discussion on how the evolving role of design professionals is reshaping salary structures within the industry, with a focus on the future job market and potential career paths for upcoming professionals.

4.2 Drafting New Laws: Overcoming Professional Association Resistance

As Building Design Science challenges traditional norms, the legal landscape becomes a crucial area of focus. This section explores the efforts and challenges in drafting new laws that accommodate the innovative nature of Building Design Science while overcoming resistance from established professional associations.

Navigating the Legal Landscape: An in-depth look at the current legal challenges and barriers to the integration of Building Design Science principles. This includes an analysis of existing laws and regulations that may hinder the adoption of new practices.

Collaborative Lawmaking: The importance of collaborative efforts between lawmakers, professional bodies, and Building Design Scientists in drafting new laws. This section will highlight successful instances where such collaboration has led to effective legal frameworks supporting multidisciplinary practices.

Case Studies in Legal Reform: Detailed case studies of jurisdictions that have successfully navigated legal reforms to accommodate the emerging role of the Hypertect. These examples will serve as models for other regions looking to implement similar changes.

Overcoming Resistance: Strategies and approaches for overcoming resistance from traditional professional bodies. This will include discussions on lobbying, advocacy, and public awareness campaigns that highlight the benefits of the new profession.

4.3 Global Competition: The Race for Implementation

The adoption of Building Design Science has sparked a global competition among countries and regions. This section examines the race to implement these principles and the factors driving this international contest.

International Adoption Trends: An analysis of how different countries are adopting Building Design Science principles. This includes a look at the economic, technological, and societal factors motivating these countries.

Leadership in Innovation: Profiles of regions that are leading the way in implementing Building Design Science. This will include insights into their strategies, the challenges they've faced, and the outcomes of their efforts.

Impact on Global Markets: An exploration of how this global race is affecting the international architecture and engineering markets, including changes in project management, client expectations, and design trends.

Future Predictions: Speculations on future developments in the global adoption of Building Design Science, including potential technological advancements and shifts in international market dynamics.

4.4 The Obituary of Traditional Firms: Rise of the Hypertect

In this transformative era, traditional architectural and engineering firms face significant challenges, making way for the rise of Hypertect-led firms. This section discusses the decline of traditional practices and the ascendancy of the new model.

Challenges for Traditional Firms: An analysis of the challenges and limitations faced by traditional design firms in adapting to the new paradigm. This includes technological, educational, and structural challenges.

Success Stories of Hypertect Firms: Detailed accounts of Hypertect-led firms that have successfully adapted to the changing landscape. This will include their strategies, the challenges they overcame, and the advantages they've gained.

Transformation of Industry Practices: A discussion on how the rise of Hypertects is transforming industry practices, from project management to client engagement and final construction.

Looking Ahead: Predictions and insights into the future of architectural and engineering firms in the context of the growing influence of Building Design Science. This will include potential paths for traditional firms to evolve and integrate the new practices.

Conclusion of Chapter 4:

Chapter 4 concludes by emphasizing the profound impact of Building Design Science on the professional landscape of architecture and engineering. From the financial implications of higher salaries and cost efficiencies to the legal challenges and global competition, the chapter paints a comprehensive picture of an industry in transformation. The rise of the Hypertect and the decline of traditional firms mark a significant shift in the industry, heralding a future where multidisciplinary expertise, technological integration, and innovative practices become the norm. This chapter sets the stage for an in-depth exploration of how these changes are reshaping the built environment and the professionals who shape it.

CHAPTER 5

Chapter 5: Real-time Awareness and Testing

5.1 Real-time Implications: Understanding Design Choices

In the dynamic field of Building Design Science, real-time awareness revolutionizes how professionals understand and implement design choices. This section delves into the multifaceted implications of having instant feedback and data at every stage of the design process.

Enhancing Decision-Making with Instant Feedback: Explore how real-time data analytics enable architects and engineers to make informed decisions quickly. This part includes examples of software and tools that provide instantaneous feedback on design elements like structural integrity, energy efficiency, and aesthetic appeal.

Adapting Designs to Changing Conditions: Discuss how real-time data allows for the adaptation of designs to changing environmental conditions, user feedback, and project requirements. This section will showcase case studies where such adaptive designs have led to successful project outcomes.

Interactive Design Process: Elaborate on the shift from a static to a dynamic design process, where real-time data fosters an interactive environment. This interaction not only occurs among the design team members but also extends to clients and stakeholders, enhancing transparency and collaboration.

Impact on Project Efficiency and Sustainability: Analyze how real-time awareness contributes to project efficiency, reducing the time and resources spent on revisions, and enhancing the sustainability of the final design.

5.2 Quantum Computing and Simulation: Testing Designs Against Millions of Scenarios

The integration of quantum computing into Building Design Science opens up unprecedented possibilities in simulation and testing. This expanded section explores the transformative potential of quantum computing in creating sophisticated simulations.

Quantum Computing in Simulating Complex Environments: Discuss the capabilities of quantum computing in simulating complex architectural environments, factoring in variables like weather patterns, seismic activity, and urban dynamics.

Advanced Scenario Testing: Delve into how quantum computing allows for testing designs against millions of scenarios in real-time, providing insights that were previously unattainable. This section includes examples of how such testing has influenced design decisions.

Design Optimization through Quantum Simulations: Examine how quantum simulations lead to optimized building designs that are more resilient, sustainable, and suited to their intended use.

Future Prospects of Quantum Computing in Architecture: Speculate on the future developments of quantum computing in building design, including potential breakthroughs and challenges in fully integrating this technology.

5.3 Smart Building Facility Maintenance: Incorporating Real-time Data

The role of real-time data extends beyond the design and construction phases into the realm of facility maintenance. This section explores the integration of real-time data in managing and maintaining smart buildings.

Predictive Maintenance Strategies: Explain how real-time data from embedded sensors and IoT devices is used in predictive maintenance, foreseeing and addressing potential issues before they escalate.

Optimizing Building Performance: Discuss how continuous data streams are analyzed to optimize building performance in areas like energy consumption, space utilization, and environmental impact.

Case Studies in Smart Facility Maintenance: Present real-life examples of buildings that have successfully implemented smart maintenance systems, highlighting the benefits and challenges faced.

Role of AI in Facility Management: Explore the growing role of AI in analyzing maintenance data, predicting future needs, and automating certain maintenance tasks.

5.4 Code Compliance: Staying Ahead of Regulations

In the rapidly evolving landscape of building regulations, staying ahead is crucial. This section addresses how real-time awareness and advanced technologies assist professionals in maintaining compliance with changing codes and standards.

Navigating the Regulatory Landscape: Discuss the complexities of current building codes and how real-time data helps professionals stay compliant, especially in jurisdictions with frequently changing regulations.

Proactive Compliance Strategies: Explore strategies and tools that enable designers and builders to proactively meet regulatory requirements, reducing the risk of non-compliance.

Role of Technology in Ensuring Compliance: Examine the role of various technologies, including AI and BIM, in simplifying the compliance process, from design to construction and operation.

Future Trends in Building Regulations: Anticipate future trends in building regulations, especially considering environmental and safety concerns, and how professionals can prepare to meet these evolving standards.

Conclusion of Chapter 5:

Chapter 5 concludes by underscoring the pivotal role of real-time awareness and advanced computing technologies in modern Building Design Science. From the impact of instant feedback on design decisions to the sophisticated simulations enabled by quantum computing, and the proactive approach to building maintenance and regulatory compliance, this chapter paints a comprehensive picture of an industry embracing dynamism, precision, and foresight. These technological advancements herald a new era in architecture and engineering, emphasizing the transformative power of real-time awareness in shaping the future of the built environment.

CHAPTER 6

Chapter 6: The Role of Jurisdictions

6.1 Pioneering Jurisdictions: A Global Race

The advent of Building Design Science has ignited a global race among jurisdictions, each vying to establish themselves as pioneers in this revolutionary field. This extensive section delves into the motivations, strategies, and impacts of this international competition.

Motivations Driving the Global Race: Analyze the various factors motivating jurisdictions to lead in Building Design Science. These include economic growth, technological advancement, environmental sustainability, and the desire to set new standards in the construction industry.

Leading Jurisdictions and Their Strategies: Provide in-depth profiles of jurisdictions that have taken significant strides in Building Design Science. Explore their strategic approaches, including investments in education, technology, and infrastructure, and how these strategies are shaping their construction industries.

Impact on Global Architectural Trends: Discuss how this race is influencing global architectural trends, with a focus on emerging design philosophies, sustainability practices, and the integration of advanced technologies in building design.

Challenges and Opportunities: Examine the challenges these pioneering jurisdictions face, such as balancing innovation with traditional practices, and the opportunities that arise from being at the forefront of Building Design Science.

6.2 Regulatory Challenges: Breaking Down Barriers

As Building Design Science evolves, it encounters significant regulatory challenges. This section explores the complexities of adapting existing regulatory frameworks to accommodate the innovative nature of Building Design Science.

Navigating Existing Regulatory Frameworks: Delve into the current regulatory landscape and its challenges in accommodating new practices in Building Design Science. This includes a discussion on safety standards, professional accreditation, and the allocation of responsibilities in collaborative projects.

The Role of Governments and Regulatory Bodies: Explore the role governments and regulatory bodies play in facilitating or hindering the growth of Building Design Science. Discuss initiatives and reforms that are being proposed or implemented to support this new field.

Case Studies of Regulatory Evolution: Present case studies from different jurisdictions where regulatory reforms have successfully integrated Building Design Science principles, highlighting the processes and outcomes of these reforms.

Strategies for Overcoming Resistance: Offer insights into strategies for overcoming resistance from traditional professional associations and regulatory bodies. This may include lobbying efforts, public awareness campaigns, and the demonstration of the efficacy and benefits of Building Design Science.

6.3 Hypertect Firms: A New Era in Design and Construction

With the rise of Building Design Science, Hypertect firms emerge as the new vanguard in the design and construction industry. This section discusses how these firms are leading a new era in building design.

Defining the Hypertect Firm: Outline what constitutes a Hypertect firm, emphasizing their multidisciplinary nature, their embrace of technology, and their approach to sustainable and efficient design.

Transformation of Industry Practices: Analyze how Hypertect firms are transforming traditional practices in the industry. This includes changes in project management, client engagement, and the overall approach to building design and construction.

Case Studies of Successful Hypertect Firms: Present detailed case studies of successful Hypertect firms, illustrating their methods, the challenges they have overcome, and the impacts they have had on the industry.

Future Prospects for Hypertect Firms: Discuss the future landscape for Hypertect firms. Speculate on potential challenges they may face, such as evolving technologies and changing market demands, and the opportunities that lie ahead.

Conclusion of Chapter 6:

Chapter 6 wraps up by highlighting the critical role that jurisdictions play in the advancement of Building Design Science. From the global competition to establish leadership in this field to the regulatory challenges that need to be navigated, and the rise of Hypertect firms reshaping the industry, this chapter paints a comprehensive picture of a sector in the midst of transformation. It underscores the importance of adaptability, collaboration, and innovation in navigating the changing landscape of design and construction, and how these elements are crucial in shaping the future of our built environment.

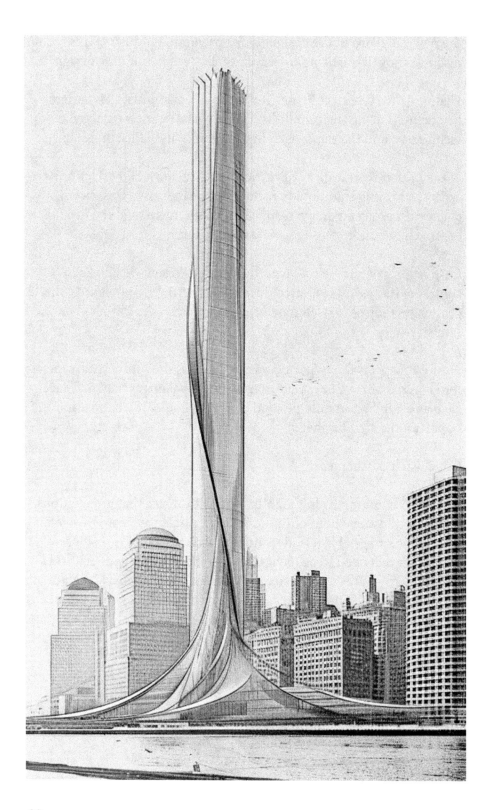

HYPERTECT BY EARL S BELL

CHAPTER 7

Chapter 7: Building Science Data Center

7.1 Infrastructure of the Future: The Importance of Dedicated Building Science Data Centers

In the advancing field of Building Design Science, the establishment of dedicated Building Science Data Centers is pivotal. This section explores their critical role as the backbone of modern architectural and engineering practices.

Centralizing Data for Enhanced Efficiency: Delve into how these data centers centralize vast amounts of information, streamlining processes from design conception to construction. Discuss the advantages of having a centralized repository for all project-related data, including ease of access, improved communication, and enhanced coordination among different stakeholders.

Advanced Data Processing Capabilities: Analyze the advanced data processing capabilities of these centers, which allow for handling complex computations, simulations, and analyses essential in modern building design. This includes the use of sophisticated software and hardware capable of processing large datasets generated by various design tools and technologies.

Scalability and Flexibility: Discuss the scalability and flexibility of Building Science Data Centers, which are crucial in adapting to the evolving needs of the construction industry. This includes their ability to integrate new technologies and methodologies as they emerge, ensuring that the infrastructure remains at the cutting edge.

Impact on Design and Construction: Explore the overall impact of these data centers on the design and construction process, highlighting how they contribute to more efficient, accurate, and sustainable building practices.

7.2 AI Infrastructure: Nurturing the Growth of Building Science Technology

Artificial Intelligence (AI) infrastructure within Building Science Data Centers is a driving force in the evolution of Building Design Science. This section examines how AI is nurtured and leveraged within these centers.

Integration of AI in Building Design: Discuss the integration of AI algorithms in building design and analysis, including their role in predictive modeling, generative design, and decision-making processes. Highlight how AI is used to interpret complex data and provide insights that would be beyond the scope of traditional methods.

Enhancing Design with Machine Learning and Analytics: Dive into the specifics of how machine learning and data analytics are used to enhance design processes. Include examples of AI-driven tools that have revolutionized areas such as energy efficiency modeling, structural analysis, and environmental impact assessment.

Continuous Development and Improvement: Address the ongoing development and improvement of AI within these centers. Discuss the processes of updating AI algorithms, training models with new data, and the continuous cycle of feedback and refinement that drives innovation.

Case Studies: Provide case studies of specific projects where AI infrastructure within Building Science Data Centers has significantly contributed to successful outcomes, demonstrating the practical applications and benefits of this technology.

7.3 Collaborative Innovation: The Heart of Building Science Data Centers

The collaborative innovation fostered within Building Science Data Centers is a cornerstone of their success. This section delves into the collaborative ecosystem that these centers support.

Facilitating Multidisciplinary Collaboration: Explore how these centers facilitate collaboration between various professionals, including architects, engineers, data scientists, and technologists. Discuss the digital platforms and communication tools that enable seamless interaction and exchange of ideas.

Innovation Through Diversity of Perspectives: Highlight the importance of having diverse perspectives in the innovation process. Discuss how bringing together experts from different fields leads to more comprehensive solutions and creative problem-solving.

Real-time Collaboration and Problem-solving: Describe the real-time collaboration capabilities provided by these data centers, allowing teams to work together in virtual environments, regardless of physical location. This includes the use of collaborative software that enables real-time design modifications and decision-making.

Innovative Project Examples: Provide examples of innovative projects that have been realized through the collaborative efforts within Building Science Data Centers. These examples should showcase how collaboration leads to breakthroughs in design and construction.

7.4 Ensuring Security and Ethical Use: A Responsible Approach

In an age where data is invaluable, ensuring the security and ethical use of information within Building Science Data Centers is paramount. This section addresses the strategies and practices implemented to maintain the integrity and security of data.

Implementing Robust Security Protocols: Discuss the implementation of robust security protocols to protect sensitive data within these centers. This includes cybersecurity measures, access controls, encryption technologies, and regular security audits.

Ethical Considerations in Data Usage: Delve into the ethical considerations involved in handling large datasets, particularly concerning privacy, consent, and data sharing. Discuss the ethical guidelines and standards that govern the use of data in building design and construction.

Compliance with Data Regulations: Explore how Building Science Data Centers ensure compliance with national and international data regulations. Discuss the challenges and strategies involved in navigating the complex landscape of data legislation.

Balancing Innovation with Responsibility: Conclude the section by discussing the balance between driving innovation through data use and maintaining a responsible and ethical approach. Highlight the importance of this balance in building trust among stakeholders and ensuring the long-term sustainability of these data centers.

Conclusion of Chapter 7:

Chapter 7 concludes by underscoring the integral role of Building Science Data Centers in the future of Building Design Science. From serving as hubs of innovation and collaboration to ensuring the security and ethical use of data, these centers are foundational in driving the industry forward. The chapter highlights the transformative impact of these centers on architectural and engineering practices, emphasizing their role in enabling more integrated, efficient, and responsible approaches to building design. The future depicted in this chapter is one where data-driven decision-making, powered by advanced infrastructure and collaborative innovation, becomes the standard in shaping our built environment.

CHAPTER 8

Chapter 8: The Future Unleashed

8.1 The Legacy of the Hypertect

The Hypertect, as a new breed of professional in the realm of Building Design Science, stands at the forefront of a transformative era in architecture and engineering. This extensive section delves into the enduring legacy that Hypertects are poised to leave in the industry.

Redefining Professional Roles: Explore how the Hypertect is redefining traditional roles within architecture and engineering. Discuss the expanded skill set and interdisciplinary knowledge that set the Hypertect apart and how this is influencing industry standards and expectations.

Impact on Design and Construction Practices: Analyze the profound impact that Hypertects have on design and construction practices. Include discussions on innovative design methodologies, sustainable practices, and the integration of new technologies such as AI and BIM in everyday work.

Influence Beyond the Industry: Consider the broader influence of the Hypertect on society, urban planning, and environmental sustainability. Discuss how the holistic approach of the Hypertect contributes to more sustainable, efficient, and human-centric urban environments.

Case Studies of Hypertect-led Projects: Present detailed case studies of groundbreaking projects led by Hypertects, showcasing their innovative approaches, the challenges they overcame, and the lasting impact of their work.

8.2 Shaping Tomorrow: The Unprecedented Impact of Building Design Science

Building Design Science, with its innovative methodologies and advanced technological integration, is set to have an unprecedented impact on the future of the built environment. This section explores the far-reaching consequences of this paradigm shift.

Revolutionizing Building Design: Delve into how Building Design Science is revolutionizing the process of building design, from conceptualization to execution. Discuss the innovative design solutions that are now possible, including adaptive and intelligent buildings that respond to environmental and user needs.

Sustainability and Environmental Impact: Focus on the impact of Building Design Science on sustainability and environmental stewardship. Explore how these practices are leading to greener, more energy-efficient, and sustainable building projects.

Transforming Urban Landscapes: Discuss the potential of Building Design Science to transform urban landscapes. Include insights into how these practices can contribute to smarter, more livable cities, and address challenges such as urban density, resource management, and environmental resilience.

Predictions for the Future: Offer predictions and forward-looking scenarios for the future of Building Design Science. Speculate on potential technological advancements, industry trends, and the evolving role of professionals in this field.

8.3 A Call to Action: Embracing the Future

As Building Design Science continues to evolve, there is a growing need for professionals, policymakers, educators, and industry leaders to embrace and drive forward this transformative approach. This section serves as a call to action for all stakeholders involved.

Encouraging Interdisciplinary Collaboration: Highlight the importance of interdisciplinary collaboration in driving the field of Building Design Science forward. Discuss how breaking down silos and fostering cooperation among different disciplines is crucial for innovation.

Role of Education and Continuous Learning: Emphasize the role of education in preparing the next generation of professionals for the challenges and opportunities presented by Building Design Science. Discuss the need for evolving educational curriculums, continuous learning, and professional development in this dynamic field.

Support from Policy and Governance: Address the need for supportive policies and governance structures that facilitate the adoption and growth of Building Design Science. Discuss how regulatory bodies and governments can play a pivotal role in creating an environment conducive to innovation and growth.

Inspiring Stories of Change and Adaptation: Conclude with inspiring stories of individuals, organizations, and communities that have embraced Building Design Science. Highlight how they are actively working to bring about change and adaptation in their fields, serving as examples for others to follow.

Conclusion of Chapter 8:

Chapter 8 concludes by painting a vivid picture of the transformative potential of Building Design Science and the pivotal role of the Hypertect in shaping this future. It underscores the importance of embracing a multidisciplinary, innovative approach to design and construction that transcends traditional boundaries. The chapter challenges all stakeholders to actively participate in this evolution, fostering a future where innovation, sustainability, and efficiency are not just aspirations but realities in the built environment. The future of Building Design Science, as envisioned in this chapter, is a dynamic interplay of human creativity, technological advancement, and visionary thinking, poised to redefine our interaction with and within the spaces we inhabit.

THE HYPERTECT

www.ingramcontent.com/pod-product-compliance
Lightning Source LLC
LaVergne TN
LVHW051634050326
832903LV00033B/4751